# Stars

Shelly C. Buchanan, M.S.

## Consultant

**Sean Goebel, M.S.**
University of Hawaii
Institute for Astronomy

## Publishing Credits

Rachelle Cracchiolo, M.S.Ed., *Publisher*
Conni Medina, M.A.Ed., *Managing Editor*
Diana Kenney, M.A.Ed., NBCT, *Content Director*
Dona Herweck Rice, *Series Developer*
Robin Erickson, *Multimedia Designer*
Timothy Bradley, *Illustrator*

**Image Credits:** Cover, pp.1, 7, 9, 11, 18, 19, 25, 27
(background), Back cover NASA; pp.5, 7, 19 (background),
23-24 iStock; p.6 (illustration) Stephanie McGinley; p.7
ESA/Hubble and NASA; p.9 (background) NASA, ESA,
and A. Feild (STSci); p.11 (top) Science Source; p.13
(background) U.S. Civilian/NASA, (bottom) NASA/JPL-
Caltech/T. Megeath (University of Toledo); p.16 Hubble/
NASA; p.17 NASA/JPL-Caltech/R. Hurt [SSC]; p.19 NASA,
ESO, NAOJ, Giovanni Paglioli; p.20 Hubble/NASA; p.27
Newscom; p.28-29 (illustration) Timothy Bradley; all other
images from Shutterstock.

### Library of Congress Cataloging-in-Publication Data

Buchanan, Shelly, author.
  Stars / Shelly C. Buchanan.
    pages cm
  Summary: 'Stars light up the sky on a clear night. They
may look the same from Earth, but they come in many
sizes and colors. Some stars are closer to Earth than
others. Some are old and some are young. Even though
stars are so far away, learning about them helps us to
better understand the world around us."-- Provided by
publisher.
  Audience: Grades 4 to 6
  Includes index.
  ISBN 978-1-4807-4728-9 (pbk.)
  1. Stars--Juvenile literature. I. Title.
  QB801.7.B83 2016
  523.8--dc23
                            2015003155

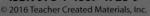

## Teacher Created Materials

5301 Oceanus Drive
Huntington Beach, CA 92649-1030
http://www.tcmpub.com

**ISBN 978-1-4807-4728-9**

# Table of Contents

# Starstruck

Have you ever looked up at the night sky and been amazed by the scattered twinkling lights? You are not alone! People have been captivated by the stars for thousands of years. Some were so starstruck that they studied their every move.

Early stargazers learned the stars could provide useful information. Ancient Egyptians planned their lives around Sirius, the Dog Star. Egyptian farmers knew they could plant crops in the moist soil after Sirius rose in the sky. The ancient Phoenicians (fi-NEE-shuhnz) navigated the seas using the night sky. They learned the annual patterns of the stars. At certain times of the year, the sun and the stars would be at fixed distances from the horizon. They used their fingers to measure the stars' positions. The Greeks named the stars after gods, heroes, and animals from their stories. The Chinese from the Han Dynasty grouped the **constellations** by the four directions—East (Dragon), West (Tiger), North (Tortoise), and South (Scarlet Bird). The Native American Tewa tribe named the Milky Way the "Endless Trail." They saw the constellation Orion as Long Sash, a hero who led his people away from their troubles on the Endless Trail.

Astronomy is the study of things in space. Many people get astronomy confused with astrology. Astronomy is based in science, while astrology is not.

# Navigation

Ancient and modern navigators have used stars and fascinating tools to guide their travels at night. The kamal is an early device that measures **latitude**. The astrolabe (AS-truh-leyb) is used to locate and predict positions of the sun, moon, planets, and stars. The sextant is one-sixth of a circle and measures the angle between an object in the sky and the horizon.

kamal

astrolabe

sextant

Modern day **astronomers** use powerful telescopes to see stars. They also use **satellites**. Computers and other instruments help scientists learn what stars are made of, how far away they are, and much more.

Astronomers have learned there are different kinds of stars. Some are hundreds of times larger than our sun, while others are much smaller. Stars come in a range of colors: blue, red, orange, yellow, and white. Their temperatures and distances from Earth range widely as well. Some stars are closer to Earth than others. The sun is our closest star.

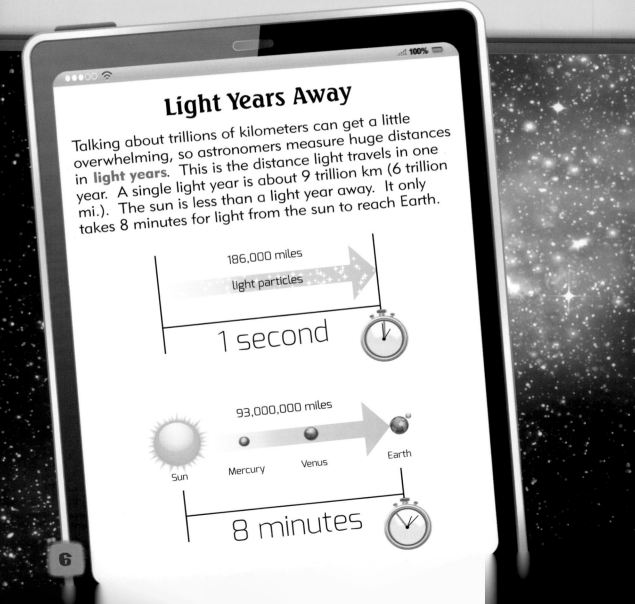

# Light Years Away

Talking about trillions of kilometers can get a little overwhelming, so astronomers measure huge distances in **light years**. This is the distance light travels in one year. A single light year is about 9 trillion km (6 trillion mi.). The sun is less than a light year away. It only takes 8 minutes for light from the sun to reach Earth.

186,000 miles

light particles

1 second

93,000,000 miles

Sun

Mercury

Venus

Earth

8 minutes

By studying the sun, astronomers have learned many things about stars. The sun is about 150 million kilometers (93 million miles) away. Flying in a jet plane, it would take you 17 years to get to the sun! The next closest star is Proxima Centauri, at a whopping 40 trillion km (25 trillion mi.) away. Many other stars are even farther away than Proxima Centauri. Despite their vast distance from us, those twinkling stars continue to fascinate us.

Stars are old! Most stars are between 1 and 10 billion years old.

## Step Back in Time

Proxima Centauri is four light years away from Earth. This means that the light we see from it is four years old. Other stars are billions of light years away. Light left the stars billions of years ago, and it is just reaching us. Some of these stars may have already burned out. Looking at stars is like looking back in time.

# Science of Stars

Over the years, astronomers have been challenged to learn more about stars. Since stars are light years away, this is a difficult task. Research shows that stars are huge balls of burning hot gases. The main chemical elements that make up stars are hydrogen and helium. These elements form clouds and collapse into stars due to **gravity**. Astronomers are still learning about stars and are trying to figure out ways to organize their information.

## Classifying Stars

In order for people to understand and learn more about stars, astronomers define and classify them. They group stars by their size and by their temperature. Stars that are the size of the sun or smaller are called **dwarfs**. Stars that are 10 times the size of the sun are called *giants*. **Supergiants** are hundreds of times larger than the sun.

To your eye alone, stars may look completely white. But when seen through a telescope, we can see that stars come in many colors. The color is related to a star's temperature. The hottest stars appear blue, and the coolest are red. There are also white, yellow, and orange stars.

### Always Shining

Stars are out all the time. We just can't see them during the day because the sun's light blocks them from view. Look at a star chart, a smartphone app, or the Internet to find out which stars we could see if we could turn off the sun's light.

# Twins!

Sometimes, one star turns out to be two stars. The stars orbit each other and are called *binary stars*. Often, one star is much larger or brighter than the other. Astronomers can find the second star by observing its "wobble." As the stars orbit each other, each star's gravity pulls on the other, causing it to wobble back and forth. Astronomers also look to see if a star drifts from time to time as another star passes in front of it.

blue-white supergiant

sun

red dwarf

red giant

Supergiant stars have a shorter lifespan than other stars, around 10–50 million years. The larger a star is, the shorter its life will be.

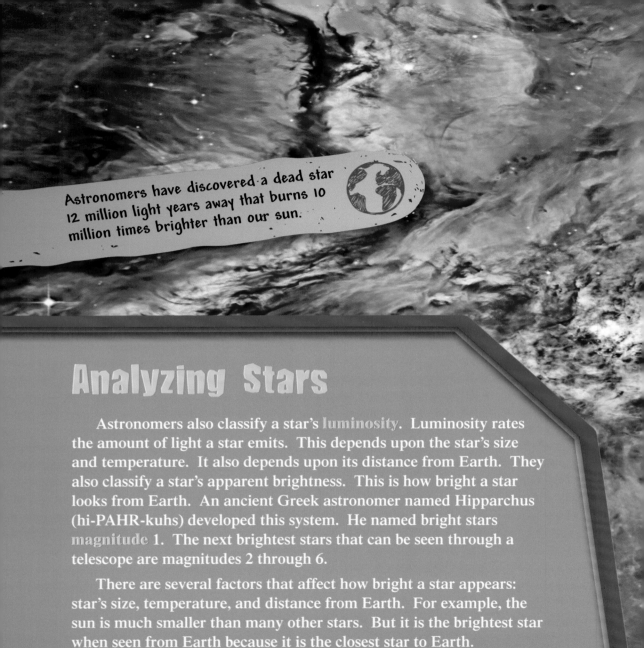

Astronomers have discovered a dead star 12 million light years away that burns 10 million times brighter than our sun.

# Analyzing Stars

Astronomers also classify a star's luminosity. Luminosity rates the amount of light a star emits. This depends upon the star's size and temperature. It also depends upon its distance from Earth. They also classify a star's apparent brightness. This is how bright a star looks from Earth. An ancient Greek astronomer named Hipparchus (hi-PAHR-kuhs) developed this system. He named bright stars magnitude 1. The next brightest stars that can be seen through a telescope are magnitudes 2 through 6.

There are several factors that affect how bright a star appears: star's size, temperature, and distance from Earth. For example, the sun is much smaller than many other stars. But it is the brightest star when seen from Earth because it is the closest star to Earth.

Astronomers also use measurements to determine the chemical makeup of stars. Even though a star may be classified as having a certain color, when its light is shown through a spectrograph, it splits into a spectrum of colors. Each star has a different spectrum. Astronomers can read the spectrum to determine each star's makeup.

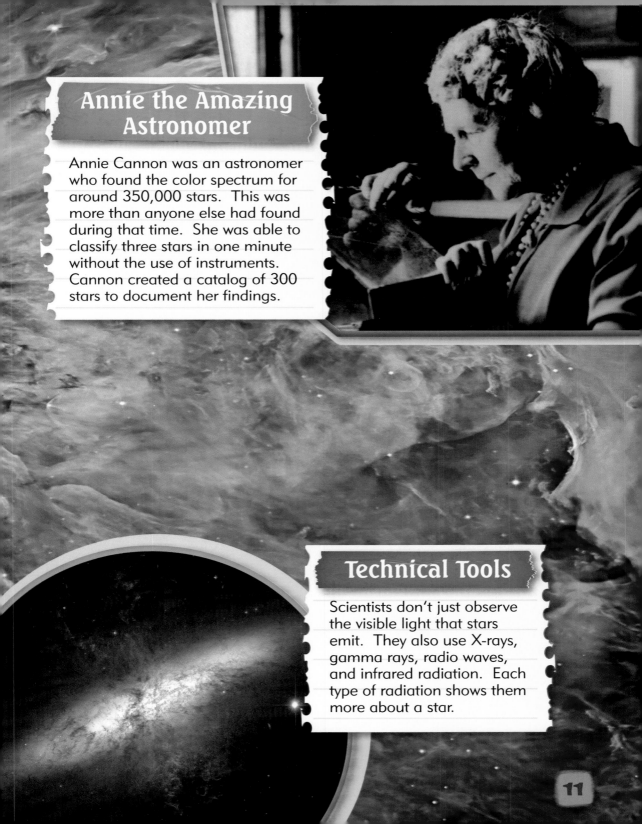

## Annie the Amazing Astronomer

Annie Cannon was an astronomer who found the color spectrum for around 350,000 stars. This was more than anyone else had found during that time. She was able to classify three stars in one minute without the use of instruments. Cannon created a catalog of 300 stars to document her findings.

## Technical Tools

Scientists don't just observe the visible light that stars emit. They also use X-rays, gamma rays, radio waves, and infrared radiation. Each type of radiation shows them more about a star.

# Star Saga

Stars are not living things, but astronomers often talk about them as though they were. The story of a star is one of balance. Gravity and the energy a star creates play tug-of-war with the star. Eventually, one of these forces must win.

## A Star Is Born

Stars begin as giant clouds of gas and dust called **nebulae**. They are mostly made of hydrogen gas. These huge clouds are like star nurseries. One nebula can produce hundreds sometimes even thousands of stars.

Slowly, gravity pulls gas and dust from the nebula together into clumps. As the clump gathers, its gravity grows stronger. This draws in more gas and dust, and the clump begins to spin. Over the course of about one hundred thousand years, the spinning cloud gets hotter and thicker. Finally, it gets so thick that it collapses into a ball, called a **protostar**. The dust and gas gather together as the center heats up. When the center reaches 15 million degrees Celsius (27 million degrees Fahrenheit), **nuclear fusion** begins. As the core of the protostar begins to burn, a star is born!

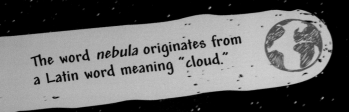

The word *nebula* originates from a Latin word meaning "cloud."

Planets, comets, and asteroids are also formed from spinning clouds of gas and dust.

Tarantula Nebula

protostars

Orion Nebula

13

# Balancing Act

Once nuclear fusion begins in a star's core, it is considered a *main sequence star*. This is the stage in which a star spends 80–90 percent of its life. The fusion in the core of a star generates a massive amount of heat and energy. This pushes the star outward and stops gravity from collapsing it any further. The star is now balanced between the outward pressure released by nuclear fusion and the inward pull of its own gravity. These balanced forces keep a star about the same size for the entire main sequence stage, making this stage of the star's life the most stable.

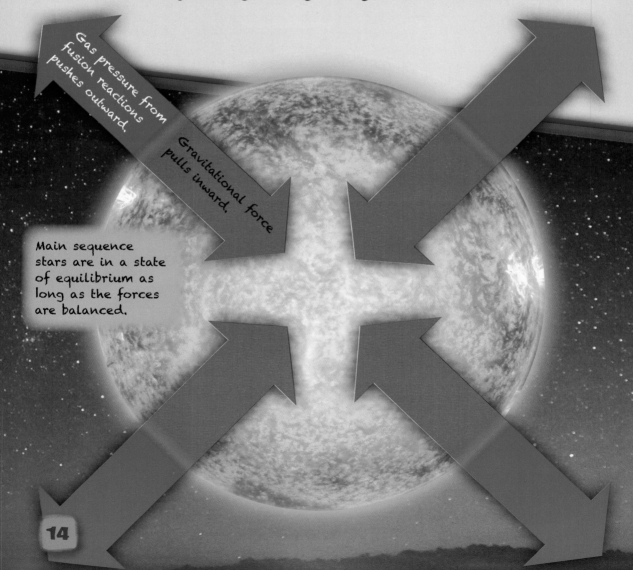

Gas pressure from fusion reactions pushes outward.

Gravitational force pulls inward.

Main sequence stars are in a state of equilibrium as long as the forces are balanced.

A star will remain in its main sequence stage for as long as it has hydrogen to fuse. This is different for different-size stars. Large stars have more hydrogen, but they burn through it much faster than smaller, more efficient stars. The largest stars actually have the shortest lives.

Eventually, their supply of hydrogen dwindles. All stars will run out of fuel. But their deaths can be even more spectacular than their lives.

## Nuclear Fusion

Nuclear fusion powers stars. Deep inside the core of a star, hydrogen atoms smash together with great force. They fuse to make helium atoms. This releases an enormous amount of energy and light. This is why we can see stars that are so far away.

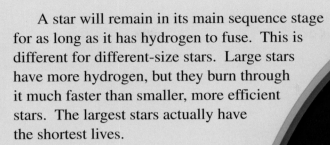

hydrogen atoms

helium atom

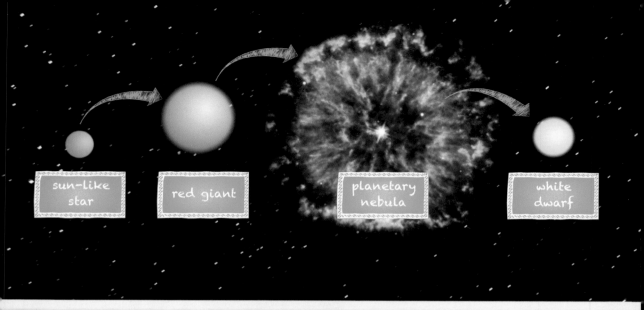

sun-like star

red giant

planetary nebula

white dwarf

# Violent Deaths

With no more fuel to burn, fusion in the core of a star stops, and gravity begins to win the stellar tug-of-war. But the death of a star depends on its size. Smaller stars collapse into themselves and become extremely dense white dwarfs. Medium-size stars, like our sun, expand to become red giants. After a few hundred thousand years, their outer layers expand outward, leaving behind their cores as white dwarfs.

The death of a large star comes with terrific force and makes for quite a show! When a star 30 times the **mass** of the sun dies, it explodes into a massive **supernova**. It flings dust and particles from the star's outer layers far into space. Eventually, these star fragments get recycled. They become the building blocks in nebulae and are reborn as stars and planets.

After a supernova blast, a star may collapse into a **neutron star**. A neutron star is only a few kilometers wide. It's so dense that one spoonful of it would weigh as much as a mountain! If the star is more than 30 times the mass of the sun, the supernova turns into a **black hole**. This super-dense object has so much gravity that not even light can escape it.

## Death by Sun

Our sun is about halfway through its main sequence stage. It has another five billion years left before it runs out of fuel. But when our sun does run out of hydrogen, scientists predict that it will grow 30 times larger and give off 10 times more energy than it currently does. Consequently, the sun's heat and energy will engulf Earth.

protostar

blue supergiant

supernova

black hole

elliptical

irregular

spiral

# Galaxies

Stars collect together with other debris, gases, and dust to form **galaxies**. Gravity holds these objects together. Scientists can see far-off galaxies thanks to the light that shines from so many stars. The famous astronomer, Edwin Hubble, classified galaxies into three types—elliptical, irregular, and spiral.

## Elliptical Galaxies

Elliptical galaxies are usually round in shape. They are made only of older stars. Elliptical galaxies are not nearly as bright as spiral galaxies, and most are smaller in size. They may contain just a few thousand stars, and it's common for the stars to be close together. This can sometimes make the galaxy look like one gigantic star.

## Irregular Galaxies

Irregular galaxies are not round or spiral in shape. These galaxies are usually misshapen or formless. Scientists believe these galaxies may have once been elliptical or spiral galaxies but have lost their shape over time. They may have crashed into another galaxy, or they may be pulled out of shape by the gravity of nearby galaxies.

## This Just In!

Scientists estimate that 80 percent of the mass in space cannot be seen! Astronomers call it *dark matter*, and they think it exists in huge spaces between the stars. They believe this matter holds stars and planets in their galaxies.

Edwin Hubble wanted to give astronomers "hope to find something we had not expected."

Sombrero galaxy

## Billion, Trillion, Sextillion?

Galaxies hold hundreds of billions of stars. Scientists estimate that there are over 100 billion galaxies in the universe. Currently, NASA estimates that there are about 1,000,000,000,000,000,000,000, or 1 sextillion, stars in the universe!

# Spiral Galaxies

Spiral galaxies are shaped like pinwheels. At the center is a flat disk shape made up of older stars. Twisting arms extend from this center. The spinning motion of the arms gives the galaxy its spiral shape. The waves of the arms create very large new stars. The great light of these large stars makes the nearby dust clouds glow brightly.

Our own galaxy, the Milky Way, is a spiral galaxy. It's home to us, our sun, and another hundred billion stars. It's one hundred thousand light years across and rotates once every two hundred million years. The center is loaded with stars that surround a very large black hole. These stars stretch for fifteen thousand light years. The Milky Way is so enormous that several smaller galaxies orbit it. Talk about huge!

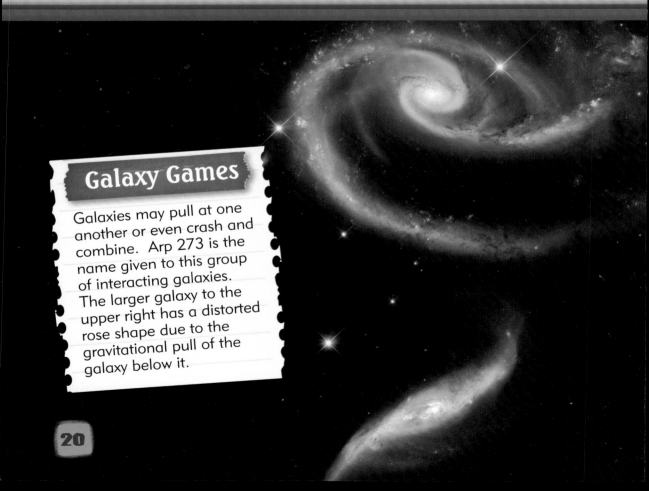

## Galaxy Games

Galaxies may pull at one another or even crash and combine. Arp 273 is the name given to this group of interacting galaxies. The larger galaxy to the upper right has a distorted rose shape due to the gravitational pull of the galaxy below it.

The center of the Milky Way is hard for astronomers to see. This is because clouds of dust and gas block their view. Scientists believe there may be a very large black hole at the center of the Milky Way. This massive black hole has super-powerful gravity. It swallows anything that wanders into its territory. It's a good thing we're thousands of light years away!

## Comparing Galaxies

Use the diagram below to compare and contrast the three different galaxies.

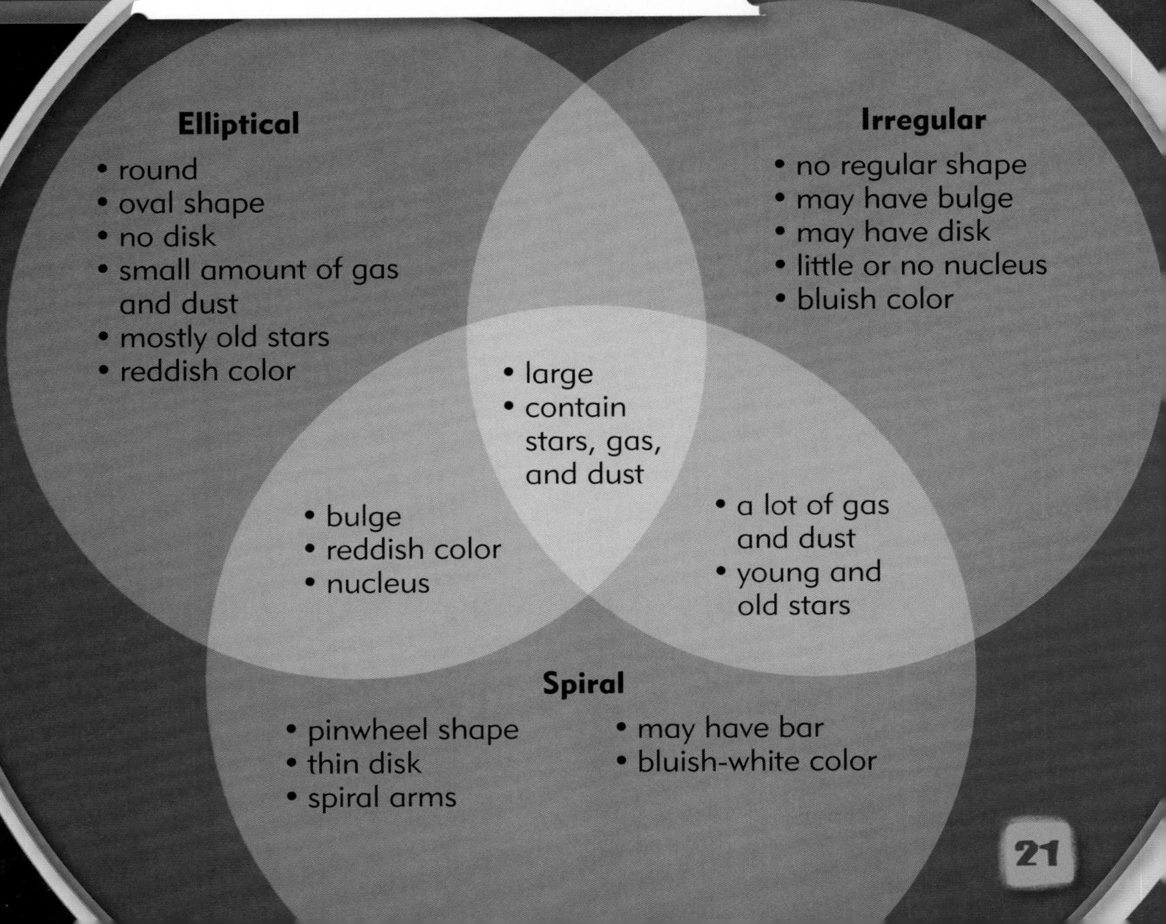

### Elliptical
- round
- oval shape
- no disk
- small amount of gas and dust
- mostly old stars
- reddish color

### Irregular
- no regular shape
- may have bulge
- may have disk
- little or no nucleus
- bluish color

- large
- contain stars, gas, and dust

- bulge
- reddish color
- nucleus

- a lot of gas and dust
- young and old stars

### Spiral
- pinwheel shape
- thin disk
- spiral arms

- may have bar
- bluish-white color

# Our Solar System

Our solar system is one tiny part of the Milky Way. Our own star, the sun, lies at the center of the solar system. All other materials revolve around the sun. As the sun was born, gases, dust, and rocks swirled around it. They crashed together to create planets, moons, asteroids, comets, and meteors.

The sun is by far the largest object in our solar system. It contains 99 percent of all the material in our solar system. The sun's gravity keeps planets, moons, and other objects in orbit.

Each of the eight planets in the solar system is unique. They have different properties, colors, and sizes. The inner planets are much smaller than the outer planets. This is because of the location of the planet when it formed and its proximity, or distance, to the sun. Heat from the sun burned up the gases of the inner planets. The outer planets, however, were farther from the sun and did not lose their gases, making them larger.

The sun sings a long, slow song that we can't hear unless we use special instruments. It sounds like a deep humming.

Lucky for us, the sun was the exact right size and distance away from Earth to allow our planet to have liquid water. Scientists think that this is one of the main reasons life was able to develop on Earth. We still rely on the sun's energy to sustain us. Our solar neighbor in space makes life possible!

## Our Planets

The chart to the right shows information for each planet in our solar system. The chart includes the length of a day and a year and the number of moons for each planet. Remember these measurements are according to our time on Earth.

| Planet | Day | Year | Moons |
|---|---|---|---|
| Mercury | 59 days | 88 days | 0 |
| Venus | 243 days | 225 days | 0 |
| Earth | 1 day | 365 days | 1 |
| Mars | 25 hours | 687 days | 2 |
| Jupiter | 10 hours | 12 years | 66 |
| Saturn | 11 hours | 29.5 years | 62 |
| Uranus | 17 hours | 84 years | 27 |
| Neptune | 16 hours | 165 years | 13 |

# Star Studies

Long ago, the sky was clear. Stars were easy to see because there were no bright city lights. Thousands of stars sparkled against the velvety blackness of night. Stargazing was popular entertainment. Today, it is much harder to see stars. Pollution and electrical lighting dim the twinkling starlight. To see many stars, we must venture outside the cities most of us call home.

Astronomers have developed powerful telescopes and special devices to see stars. These instruments allow people to see stars not visible to the naked eye. Some of these huge telescopes are larger than a school gym. Many are built in remote mountain areas far from bright city lights, where the air is clean and the night is dark. These stellar lookouts are the best places for studying stars.

Other powerful telescopes float in space. Without Earth's atmosphere, these machines are able to peer deeper into space than Earth-bound telescopes. These telescopes collect photos and other kinds of data. They help astronomers learn about thousands of distant stars and galaxies.

## Helpful Hubble

A well-known and exciting tool for star study is the Hubble Space Telescope. It may look like little more than a tin can, but it has taken some of the most striking photos of deep space. With it, astronomers have studied the births and deaths of stars. They have looked billions of light years into space.

If you look closely, you will notice that stars are not all the same color. They can be white, blue, yellow, orange, or red.

## Sun Shows

Using hi-tech equipment, we have learned much about the surface of the sun. Its surface is a fiery mass of hot gases that boil and splash. Fountains of super-heated gases shoot out and put on quite a show! Dark spots appear and disappear. Our sun, which seems so constant, is constantly changing.

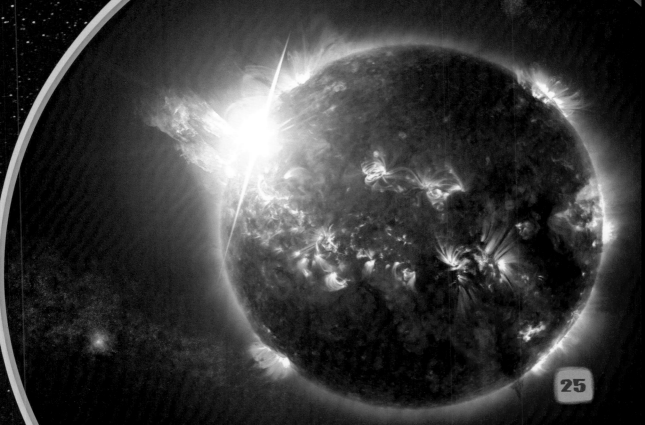

Scientists are always looking for new ways to study and explore space. They hope to learn more about how the universe began and how it has changed since then. They want to piece together the history of the universe. They are also on a quest to see if there are forms of life on other planets or if we are alone in the universe. They have identified several planets that are similar to Earth, but they're too far away for us to reach.

Astronomers and engineers are looking for new ways to power spacecraft. One idea is to use solar power. With an unlimited supply of energy from the sun, spacecrafts could travel much deeper into space.

In the meantime, you can learn about stars yourself. All you need is a clear, dark night away from city lights. Bring a star chart or use an app to help you locate stars, constellations, planets, and even galaxies. Keep studying the night sky, and maybe one day *you* will make the next great discovery.

The search for life outside of our planet is abbreviated to SETI, or Search for Extraterrestrial Intelligence.

Frank Drake

## Is There Life Beyond Ours?

Frank Drake created an equation to estimate the amount of life in our galaxy. Using this equation, scientists estimated that there might be 12,000 civilizations in our galaxy. Other scientists argue that with different numbers in the equaton, there could be only about two or three civilizations in each galaxy. Either way, the possibility exists out there.

# Think Like a Scientist

How do scientists compare light from different stars? Experiment and find out!

## What to Get

- box (cube-shaped is best)
- cardboard tube
- CD
- duct tape
- paper

- thin cardboard
- transparent, milky plastic film such as tape or a white grocery bag

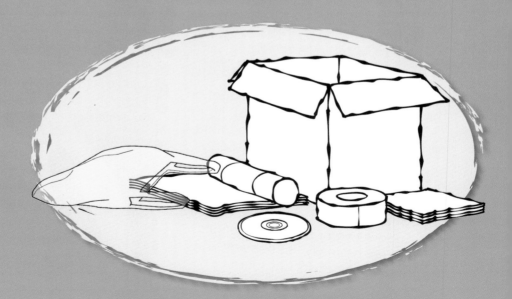

# What to Do

**1** Tape paper over most of the CD, leaving a small section uncovered.

**2** Tape the covered CD to the inside of the box. The uncovered section should be aligned with a corner of the box. Then, cut a small hole about 5 centimeters (2 inches) directly across from the uncovered section of the CD.

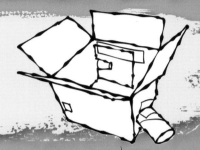

**3** Tape two thin pieces of cardboard over the hole to create a small vertical slit about 1 mm (0.04 in.) wide. Tape transparent, milky film over the slit.

**4** On the side of the box, adjacent to where the CD is exposed, cut another small hole. Tape a cardboard tube around this hole. This will be the eyepiece.

**5** Close the box and tape it closed. Shine different kinds of light through the slit and view it through the eyepiece. What do you notice? How do the light sources compare? What do you think makes them appear different?

# Glossary

**astronomers**—people who observe celestial phenomena

**black hole**—an area in space with gravity so strong that light cannot escape

**constellations**—groups of stars that form particular shapes in the sky and have been given names

**dwarfs**—stars of ordinary or low luminosity and relatively small mass and size

**galaxies**—systems of stars, gas, and dust held together by gravity

**gravity**—a force that acts between objects, pulling one toward the other

**latitude**—the position of a place measured in degrees north or south of the equator

**light years**—the distance light can travel in one year

**luminosity**—the quality or state of something producing light

**magnitude**—the size or power of something

**mass**—the amount of matter an object contains

**nebulae**—clouds of gas and dust in space

**neutron star**—a very small, dense star composed mostly of tightly packed neutrons

**nuclear fusion**—an atomic reaction in which two nuclei combine to make a larger one, releasing a large amount of energy

**protostar**—a cloud of gas and dust in space believed to develop into a star

**satellites**—objects in space that orbit other larger objects

**spectrograph**—instrument that splits light into different spectrums

**supergiants**—extremely large and luminous stars

**supernova**—explosion of a star that causes it to become extremely bright

# Index

# YOUR TURN!

## A Night Out

Go outside on a clear night. Look at the sky through an empty toilet paper roll or paper towel roll. Count the number of stars you see. Record the number. Do this several times with different patches of sky. From which location do you see the most stars? From which location do you see the least? Why do you think it is different? Share your findings with your friends and family.